The Urbana Free Library

EXPLORING
EARTHQUAKES

SEISMOLOGISTS AT WORK!

ELSIE OLSON

Consulting Editor, Diane Craig, M.A./Reading Specialist

Super Sandcastle

An Imprint of Abdo Publishing
abdopublishing.com

abdopublishing.com

Published by Abdo Publishing, a division of ABDO, PO Box 398166, Minneapolis, Minnesota 55439. Copyright © 2018 by Abdo Consulting Group, Inc. International copyrights reserved in all countries. No part of this book may be reproduced in any form without written permission from the publisher. Super SandCastle™ is a trademark and logo of Abdo Publishing.

Printed in the United States of America, North Mankato, Minnesota

102017
012018

Design: Kelly Doudna, Mighty Media, Inc.
Production: Mighty Media, Inc.
Editor: Jessie Alkire
Cover Photographs: Courtesy of the Archives, California Institute of Technology; iStockphoto
Interior Photographs: Courtesy of the Archives, California Institute of Technology; iStockphoto; Shutterstock; UNAVCO; Wikimedia Commons

Publisher's Cataloging-in-Publication Data

Names: Olson, Elsie, author.
Title: Exploring earthquakes: seismologists at work! / by Elsie Olson.
Other titles: Seismologists at work!
Description: Minneapolis, Minnesota : Abdo Publishing, 2018. | Series: Earth detectives |
Identifiers: LCCN 2017946511 | ISBN 9781532112294 (lib.bdg.) | ISBN 9781614799719 (ebook)
Subjects: LCSH: Seismology--Juvenile literature. | Earthquakes--Juvenile literature. |
    Occupations--Juvenile literature. | Earth sciences--Juvenile literature.
Classification: DDC 551.22--dc23
LC record available at https://lccn.loc.gov/2017946511

Super SandCastle™ books are created by a team of professional educators, reading specialists, and content developers around five essential components—phonemic awareness, phonics, vocabulary, text comprehension, and fluency—to assist young readers as they develop reading skills and strategies and increase their general knowledge. All books are written, reviewed, and leveled for guided reading, early reading intervention, and Accelerated Reader™ programs for use in shared, guided, and independent reading and writing activities to support a balanced approach to literacy instruction.

CONTENTS

WHAT IS AN EARTHQUAKE?

An earthquake happens when parts of Earth shake. **Seismic** waves cause this shaking. These waves start deep inside Earth.

Quakes can occur anywhere. But most happen at fault lines. These are places where pieces of Earth's **crust** fit together. Sometimes the pieces slip past one another. This causes a quake.

WHO STUDIES EARTHQUAKES?

Seismologists are scientists. They study earthquakes. They teach earthquake safety. Learning how quakes work saves many lives.

Earth has 500,000 detectable quakes per year. Some are too small to be felt by humans. Others cause great harm. They **topple** buildings. They cause **tsunamis**.

Tsunami waves can reach 100 feet (30.5 m) high!

Some seismologists do field surveys. They study the land and use equipment to measure seismic activity.

CHARLES FRANCIS RICHTER

Charles Francis Richter was a seismologist. He was born in Ohio. But he spent most of his life in California. He became interested in earthquakes in college.

Richter kept studying earthquakes after he finished school. At the time, scientists measured quakes using the Mercalli scale. It measured earthquake **damage**. But it did not measure earthquake power.

Richter went to college at Stanford University in California. He studied physics at the California Institute of Technology after graduating. Then, he taught about quakes!

THE RICHTER SCALE

Richter created a new scale. He worked with seismologist Beno Gutenberg. They invented the Richter Scale in 1935.

The scale measures the strength of **seismic** waves. A higher number means a more powerful quake. The largest known quakes were 8.9 on the Richter scale.

Beno Gutenberg

CHARLES FRANCIS RICHTER

BORN: April 26, 1900, near Hamilton, Ohio

MARRIED: Lillian Brand, July 19, 1928

CHILDREN: None

DIED: September 30, 1985, Pasadena, California

MEASURING QUAKES

Scientists have tools to study quakes as they occur. They use these tools in areas where quakes are common.

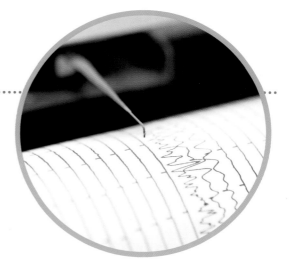

A seismograph recording waves

Machines record a quake's **seismic** waves. Scientists study these waves. They figure out where the quake began. This is the epicenter. Sometimes a small quake means a larger one is coming. Knowing a quake's location can help scientists **predict** future quakes.

Seismologists use computers and special programs to interpret data from instruments in the field, such as seismographs.

AFTER THE SHAKING

Tools exist to study quakes as they happen. But most study occurs after the events.

Seismologists study a quake's **damage**. They learn about the area's rock and soil. Waves move slower through some kinds of rock. This builds energy. It can cause more damage. Scientists ask people what the quake felt like. This gives scientists an idea of how strong the quake was.

Shaking is more powerful in sandy soil. This can turn sand into liquid! Roads and buildings can sink or collapse.

PREDICTING QUAKES

Scientists cannot **predict** earthquakes. But they can look for clues. These clues tell when a quake might be coming.

Scientists study past quakes. This shows how often quakes occur in an area. Scientists also look at earthquake **damage**. This helps them tell people how to stay safe.

Nature also gives clues about quakes. Common toads can sense quakes! They leave ponds and go to safety days before a quake.

In 2016, an earthquake destroyed much of the historic city of Amatrice in Italy.

A SEISMOLOGIST'S TOOL KIT

SEISMOGRAPH
This tool records **seismic** waves. It draws lines. The size of the lines tells how strong the quake was.

GPS
GPS measures the distance between fault locations. Scientists see if these distances change.

Seismologists use many tools to measure and record quakes.

TILTMETER
This tool measures vertical ground movement. It tells how much the ground rises or falls.

STRAINMETER
This measures changes in Earth's **crust**. It can tell if the crust is under **stress**.

QUAKE SAFETY

There is no way to stop an earthquake. But scientists teach people to stay safe during one.

Seismologists teach engineers how to make buildings stronger. Strong buildings do better in a quake. They **absorb** the shaking. Future buildings may even have sensors. These could help a building **withstand** the force of a quake.

Some engineers construct buildings with strong steel frames to withstand earthquakes.

BECOME A SEISMOLOGIST!

Do you dream of becoming a seismologist? Here are some things you can do now!

TAKE SCIENCE AND MATH CLASSES. Studying earthquakes involves math and science. Getting good grades in those classes now will help you in the future.

PRACTICE YOUR WRITING AND SPEAKING SKILLS. Seismologists often give speeches about their research. They also write a lot of papers.

ASK QUESTIONS! Scientists ask a lot of questions. They look for new ways to find answers. You can get started now!

TEST YOUR KNOWLEDGE

1. The Mercalli Scale measures earthquake **damage**. TRUE OR FALSE?

2. Who invented the Richter Scale?

3. In what year was the Richter Scale invented?

THINK ABOUT IT!

Are there earthquakes near where you live? Have you ever felt one?

ANSWERS: 1. True 2. Charles Francis Richter and Beno Gutenberg 3. 1935

GLOSSARY

absorb – to soak up or take in.

crust – the outer layer of a planet.

damage – harm or ruin.

global positioning system (GPS) – a space-based navigation system used to pinpoint locations on Earth.

predict – to guess something ahead of time on the basis of observation, experience, or reasoning.

seismic – of or relating to vibrations in the earth.

stress – strain or pressure.

topple – to become unbalanced and fall over.

tsunami – a great sea wave produced by an undersea earthquake or volcanic eruption.

withstand – to survive or resist the effect of something.